THE HOUSE OF THE GOOD NEIGHBOR

Small Acts, Big Heart:
A Manual for the Kind Revolution

By Jake Howard

Dedication

To my wife, **Jenn**, who gave me faith when I didn't know how to hold it myself.

To my mother, **Barbara**, who showed me that true empathy is quiet, steady, and brave.

To my bonus dad, **Wally**, who taught me that helping isn't about being noticed—it's about simply doing what needs to be done.

To my dad, **Steve**, who left this world far too soon—but left behind lessons that echo every day. He taught me to treat children as equals, with respect, humor, and heart.

To my daughters, Adelynn and Arabelle, who fill my world with wonder—

Adelynn, for teaching me that anything is possible if you just believe, even becoming a flower to welcome butterflies;

Arabelle, for reminding me that creativity should always come with a smile and to dress up any chance you get.

To my sister, **Shanna**, whose words have always brightened my days, and whose heart always chose to forgive me.

To my brother, **Jesse**, who showed me that mastery is worth chasing, that growth is always possible, and that we are never finished becoming.

To my **friends** who've seen the world differently than I do—thank you for challenging me with kindness. And to those who've stood beside me, echoing my hopes and doubts—thank you for reminding me I'm not alone.

And to **Mister Rogers,** whose kindness cracked open the hardest places in the world and made room for everyone to belong. This house was built, and I was built, with what you taught me. Every brick, every word, carries a piece of you. Thank you—for everything.

Take a moment—just 30 seconds—and think of a person, or even a few people, who have made a positive impact on your life. It could be a family member, a teacher, a friend (past or present), or even a stranger who noticed you at just the right time.

Go ahead. Let their faces come to mind. This book is for them. And for you.

Table of Contents

Introduction

If you're holding this book, it means you believe—or want to believe—that goodness still matters. The House of the Good Neighbor was created with that hope in mind. It's a place built not with walls, but with choices: to be kind when it's easier to turn away, to listen when it's easier to speak, to love when it's easier to judge.

This idea was inspired by Mister Rogers, who showed the world that you don't have to be famous, powerful, or loud to change lives. You just have to care—really care.

What's inside these pages isn't a rulebook or a complete guide to life. There's no way this book can cover every scenario or every challenge we face. It's a start. These are not the biggest ideas, just ones I felt might help someone, somewhere, feel a little less alone and a little more understood.

These ideas are for anyone who feels a little too small, a little too tired, or a little too heartbroken by the world, but still dares to believe that one person's kindness can make a difference. **You're not just welcome here. You're needed.**

All of us, at some time or other, need help. Whether we're giving or receiving help, each one of us has something valuable to bring to this world. That's one of the things that connects us as neighbors—in our own way, each one of us is a giver and a receiver.

- Fred Rogers

Chapter 1: Why We Build This House

This book was published in a time when the world felt like it was coming apart at the seams.

A time when racism, once whispered, returned with a roar.

A time when science and truth were twisted by power-hungry voices hiding behind the banner of religion.

A time when the loudest person with the biggest platform could change millions of lives.

A time when parts of US history were quietly removed from books, websites, and classrooms—rewriting the past to control the future.

A time when families were being separated and many felt powerless to stop it.

We are living through a moment where cruelty feels organized, well-funded, and proud of itself.

Where division is marketed like a product. Where fear is broadcast louder than hope.

It would be easy to sit down.
It would be easy to turn away.
It would be easy to let the noise win.

But we will not.

We retaliate—with strength.
We retaliate—with stubborn kindness.

We retaliate—by refusing to back down from what we know is right.

The House of the Good Neighbor is not for the passive.

It's not for the ones who say, "I'll help when it's safe."
It's not for the ones who hide behind excuses while others suffer.

It's for those who know that love is not soft.

Love is not weak.
Love is not passive.
Love, when real, is dangerous to the people who profit from hate.
Love, when real, is loud in its actions even if it's quiet in its words.

Everyone is welcome here.
Everyone—regardless of where you were born, who you love, what you look like, how you worship, or whether you worship at all —is welcome.

But not all ideas are welcome.

Hate disguised as "freedom" is not welcome.
Bigotry dressed up as "faith" is not welcome.
Lies packaged as "truth" are not welcome.

Only real love.
Only real hope.
Only real compassion, made visible through action.

That's the price of admission.
If you can carry that, there's a seat for you.

We will win.
It won't happen all at once.
It won't happen easily.

But we will win because we won't stop moving in the right direction.

We will win because truth outlasts lies. We will win because love, real love, never stays buried for long. We will win because a thousand small lights make the darkness impossible to ignore.

So get ready.

This isn't just a book.
It's a blueprint.
It's a battle cry.
It's a house that we build together—brick by stubborn brick.

Let's get to work.
The world needs better neighbors.
And we're the ones who are going to build them.

Chapter 2: The House We Build Together

There's no single act that builds a better world. No massive moment where everything suddenly shifts. No perfect day when all the small kindnesses finally stack up into something we can hold.

Real change is slower.
Quieter.

Built moment by moment, choice by choice, neighbor by neighbor. It's not built by one hero. It's built by all of us, together.

Every time you choose kindness instead of cruelty, you're laying a brick. Every time you choose patience instead of impatience, you're laying another. Every time you listen, forgive, help, welcome—you're adding to something bigger than yourself.

You might not see the whole house as it's being built. But it's real. It's growing every day. And you are part of it.

The House of the Good Neighbor isn't made of perfection.

It's made of effort.
It's made of people who show up even when it's inconvenient.

Who help even when it's messy.
Who love even when it's complicated.

It's not a place for perfect people. It's a place for people who keep trying to be better—one small, unseen act at a time.

Maybe you'll never see the results of every kindness you give. Maybe you'll never know who decided to stay because you smiled at them. Maybe you'll never know who found the courage to keep going because you held the door. But that's not the point.

The point is that goodness ripples outward, whether you see it or not. You are part of something bigger than your lifetime. Something that will outlast you. Something worth giving your life to.

The storms will keep coming.
The noise will keep rising.
The world will keep trying to convince you that kindness is naive, that patience is weakness, that hope is foolish.

Resist.
Resist by holding the door open anyway.
Resist by forgiving anyway.
Resist by making room at your table anyway.
Resist by building—brick by quiet, stubborn brick.

You won't always feel strong enough.
You won't always feel like you're making a difference.

You won't always feel seen.
But the work you do matters.

The way you move through the world matters. The way you treat strangers, neighbors, friends, and enemies matters. It all adds up. It all leaves a mark. It all builds something better than what was there before.

You are not alone in this work. There are others, quietly, steadily building beside you. People you've never met, living in neighborhoods you've never seen, choosing kindness you'll never hear about.

Together, we are raising the walls of something stronger than hate. Something sturdier than fear. Something more powerful than cynicism.

A house built on dignity, patience, courage, and hope.
A house big enough for everyone who's willing to keep building.

The House of the Good Neighbor isn't finished yet.
It probably never will be. It's a living thing, growing with every good choice we make. Every time we refuse to give up. Every time we believe that people are worth fighting for, even when it's hard.

You have a place here.
You have a part to play.
You have bricks only you can lay.

So keep showing up. Keep returning the cart. Keep making
room at the table. Keep forgiving. Keep listening.
Keep believing.

Not because it's easy.
Not because it's glamorous.
But because the world needs people like you.
People willing to build a better place, one neighbor at a
time.

Welcome to the House of the Good Neighbor.
You're not just invited.
You're needed.
You always have been.
You always will be.

Chapter 3: The Unseen Good

The world doesn't often celebrate the quiet ones.
You won't find news stories about the neighbor who leaves a meal on a grieving doorstep, or the stranger who returns a lost wallet without fanfare.

The world rarely notices the person who listens without interrupting, the person who forgives without demanding apology, or the person who returns their shopping cart even when no one is watching.

But make no mistake — these are the people who are holding the world together. Quietly. Gently. Steadily.

There is a kind of goodness that is so deep, so selfless, that it doesn't care if it is seen or rewarded.

It doesn't need a stage or applause.
It only needs a heart willing to act.
This is the unseen good.
And it is more powerful than we realize.

Our culture often mistakes loudness for strength.
The louder the voice, the bigger the platform, the more important the message must be — or so we're told.

But true goodness has never needed a megaphone.
It whispers instead of shouts. It moves in quiet spaces. It grows where pride cannot survive.

The House of the Good Neighbor was built to honor this kind of goodness. The kind you can miss if you're not paying attention.

The kind you can live your whole life believing doesn't matter — until the day you need it most.
We are here to say: it matters. It has always mattered.

And if we choose to live this way, even when no one notices, we are part of something bigger and stronger than any headline could ever capture.

Think about the moments that shaped you.
Not the awards or the grand gestures, but the small ones:

The teacher who believed in you when no one else did.
The friend who stayed on the phone through your silence.
The stranger who smiled at you when you felt invisible.

These moments didn't make the world's front pages.
They didn't trend online.
But they changed your life.
They kept you going.

Unseen goodness is the scaffolding that holds up everything else — the foundation no one notices but everyone depends on.
 It doesn't seek to be remembered.
 It seeks to remember others.

If you want to be part of the unseen good, here's the simple truth: You already are.

If you've ever done something kind without announcing it...
If you've ever encouraged someone who couldn't repay you...
If you've ever given up a little comfort to make someone else's life easier...

You are part of the invisible army that protects hope in a cynical world.

The challenge now is to keep going.
To stay kind even when it's inconvenient.
To choose compassion even when it's costly.
To trust that goodness sown quietly grows into strength you'll never fully see.

Because the truth is, most of the greatest things we build in this life are ones we never get to watch finish.
And that's okay.

This is the work of a good neighbor: to love without keeping score.
To show up without demanding recognition.
To build something better without carving your name into it.

It's not easy work.
In fact, it's some of the hardest work there is.

But it's the work that lasts.
Loud victories fade.
Quiet faithfulness endures.

Being a good neighbor isn't about being perfect.
It's about believing that every small, good thing you do
matters — even if the world never notices.
Especially if the world never notices.

One small kindness can hold up a person.
One person can hold up a family.
One family can hold up a community.
One community can change the direction of a city.
One city can shift the spirit of a nation.

It always starts small.
It always starts quietly.
It always starts unseen.

When we talk about being part of The House of the Good
Neighbor, we are talking about joining this movement of
invisible builders — people who believe that love, patience,
forgiveness, and generosity are more than just nice ideas.
They are tools for real change.

Real change never begins with shouting.
It begins with a hand reaching out.
It begins with a cart returned to its corral.

It begins with one person deciding to be better, even when no one else sees.

You will be tempted to believe your quiet efforts don't matter. You will be tempted to believe you need to make a splash to make a difference. That temptation is a lie.

The real heroes are not always the ones on the covers of magazines.

They are the ones who live lives of steady, stubborn goodness in a world that constantly tells them to quit.

You are one of them.
Keep holding doors open.
Keep speaking gently.
Keep forgiving quickly.
Keep choosing hope when it would be easier to sit down and give up.

This is how you change the world — not all at once, but one unseen, unstoppable act of kindness at a time.

In the House of the Good Neighbor, there are no small acts.
There are no forgotten kindnesses.
There are no invisible good hearts.

There are only people who decided — quietly, daily, imperfectly — that being good mattered, even when it didn't seem to.
And those people?

They are the ones who shape the world.

You don't have to be loud to be powerful.
You don't have to be famous to be important.
You don't have to be perfect to be good.

You only have to begin.

Welcome to the House of the Good Neighbor.

You belong here.

Chapter 4: Every Person Has Worth

Dignity is not earned. It's honored.

If you could see every person the way they were meant to be seen— not through the filters of appearance, wealth, success, or mistakes — you would see someone of infinite worth.

Every human life, no matter how broken, difficult, or different, carries within it the same fragile and powerful truth:
It matters.

Not because of how much it can produce.
Not because of how well it can perform.
Not because of how closely it mirrors your own.
Every person matters simply because they exist.

It sounds simple, doesn't it?
But living as if every person has worth is one of the hardest things you'll ever do.
Because sometimes people are rude.
Sometimes they're selfish.
Sometimes they make choices you can't understand.
Sometimes they hurt you.
And still—their worth doesn't vanish.

In the House of the Good Neighbor, we don't pretend hurt doesn't exist. We don't ignore reality. But we remember: dignity is not a reward for good behavior.

It is the foundation of being human.
Even when we're disappointed.

Even when we're tired.
Even when someone else's brokenness collides with ours.

It's easy to value someone who is kind to you. It's easy to celebrate those who mirror your beliefs and values. But the real test of seeing worth is how you treat the people you don't like.

The people who challenge you.
The people you find inconvenient or even exhausting.
Do they matter less?
If we're honest, many of us act like they do.

But real love says:
"You are valuable, even when you're difficult. Even when I don't understand you. Even when I'm hurt."

Real love doesn't erase boundaries.
But it refuses to erase people.

Dignity means refusing to reduce people to their worst decisions. It means believing that no human being can be summed up by a single moment of failure, anger, fear, or ignorance.

It's tempting to categorize people:
Good and bad.
Worthy and unworthy.
Us and them.

But the truth is, each of us carries both light and shadow. Each of us has made mistakes. Each of us has needed forgiveness we didn't deserve.

Dignity demands we see the full story, not just the broken chapter. It demands we see ourselves in others—especially when it's uncomfortable.

Some of the people you are called to love will never thank you. Some will never change. Some will hurt you again. Dignity doesn't mean staying in harmful relationships. It doesn't mean accepting abuse.

It means seeing that even when you must walk away, the person is still a person—not a monster. It means refusing to lose your own goodness while responding to someone else's pain.

You can set boundaries without setting fire to your own heart. You can walk away without walking into bitterness. You can protect your peace and still honor their worth.

One of the most powerful things you can ever do is to treat someone with respect when you have every excuse not to.

When you're tired.
When you're right.
When you're frustrated.
When you could get away with being cruel and no one would blame you.

Choosing dignity in those moments isn't weakness.
It's strength.

It's the kind of strength the world desperately needs—and
the kind that builds true community.
Because when you honor someone's humanity, even when
they fail, you are holding a door open. You are saying,
"You can still choose better. I believe you can be more than
this moment."

Sometimes they will walk through that door.
Sometimes they won't.
But your job isn't to control the outcome.
Your job is to keep building doors instead of walls.

Children know instinctively that they are worthy.
They don't measure their value by productivity or approval.
They exist—and they believe that is enough.
Somewhere along the way, most of us forget.

We learn that love has conditions.
We learn that belonging must be earned.
The House of the Good Neighbor exists to undo that lie.

You do not have to earn your worth.
And neither does anyone else.
We live from our worth—not for it.

When we truly believe that, everything changes.
We stop needing to prove ourselves.

We stop needing others to prove themselves to us.
We begin to see clearly again.

Imagine a world where every person was treated like they mattered.

The lonely would feel less invisible.
The angry would feel less defensive.
The broken would feel less ashamed.
The proud would feel less afraid to be vulnerable.

This isn't naïve idealism. It's a radical, practical way to heal communities, one interaction at a time. When you honor the worth of others, you change the atmosphere around you. You make it safer to be human. You create a world where people are not reduced to their mistakes, their labels, their wounds. You create a world that looks a little more like home.

In the House of the Good Neighbor, every door is open to every person—not because they are perfect, but because they are human.

You are valuable.
So is the person sitting across from you.
So is the person you disagree with.
So is the person you don't even notice yet.

This is where it all begins:

Recognizing worth.
Protecting dignity.
Living as if every encounter is holy ground.

Because it is.

Every person is a universe.
Every encounter is a chance to choose love.
This is the way of the unseen good.
This is the way of the good neighbor.
And it starts right now, right where you are.

It's easy to believe that some people are too far gone.
Too angry.
Too cruel.
Too broken.

It's tempting to write them off as lost causes.
To believe they don't deserve kindness, dignity, or hope.

But the truth is—even the people we call "evil" matter.
Even they are capable of change. Even they are more than
their worst choices.

That doesn't excuse the harm they've done.
It doesn't mean you stay close to someone who is
dangerous. It doesn't mean you let people off the hook.

It means you recognize a deeper truth: No one is beyond the possibility of becoming more than who they are right now.

If we believe that people can't change, then we also believe that we ourselves are stuck forever too.

And that is not true.

Growth is real.
Change is real.
Redemption is real—not always loud, not always public, not always immediate—but real.

Every person, no matter how lost, carries the possibility of something better inside them.

You don't have to save them.
You don't have to fix them.
But you can hold onto the stubborn belief that they matter, even when they can't see it themselves.

Sometimes just one person believing it
is enough to light the way home.

Chapter 5: Kindness Is a Daily Practice

Not a performance. Not a brand. A way of being.

Kindness isn't something you "have."
It's something you do.
Over and over.
Until it becomes how you move through the world.

It's not about being liked.
It's not about being seen.
It's not about posting it for validation.
Kindness that needs applause isn't kindness—it's
marketing.

Real kindness shows up without a stage. It happens in
kitchens and classrooms and grocery store lines. It happens
in text messages, and moments of silence, and quiet second
chances.

It happens when you take a breath instead of saying what
you want to say. It happens when you answer the phone
even though you're tired. It happens when you give
someone the grace you wish someone had given you.

Daily kindness is not dramatic.
It won't trend.
It won't always feel satisfying.
It might even go unnoticed.

But it builds something permanent.

The Myth of "Nice People"

Some people think kindness belongs to a certain kind of
person— the naturally sweet, the quiet, the soft-spoken.

But kindness is not personality.
It's not weakness.
It's a decision.
And it belongs to everyone.

You can be loud and kind.
You can be angry and kind.
You can be struggling and still choose kindness.

Don't confuse kindness with compliance.
Kindness doesn't mean agreeing with everything.
It doesn't mean accepting injustice.
It means choosing respect, even when you resist.
It means choosing humanity, even in hard conversations.

What You Practice Grows Stronger

You don't become kind all at once.
You become kind by practicing.

You practice when you're in traffic.
When you're disappointed.
When you're interrupted.
When you're right and want to win.
When you're hurt and want to hurt back.

Every time you choose to soften instead of sharpen—
you're practicing. Every time you slow down to help—
you're practicing. Every time you don't laugh at someone
else's pain — you're practicing.

Kindness is a skill.
And like any skill, it requires effort, patience, and humility.

When It's Hardest to Be Kind

Some days, kindness will feel impossible.
You'll be overwhelmed.
You'll be tired.
You'll be discouraged by how others act.

That's okay.

You don't have to be kind perfectly to be kind
meaningfully. You just have to try again.

And if you fail—if you snap, or judge, or forget—
then kindness begins again in how you treat yourself.

You don't beat yourself up for being human.
You pause.
You reflect.
You start over.

Kindness isn't about always getting it right.
It's about always coming back to love.

Kindness Changes Culture

People mirror what they experience.
When they are treated with suspicion, they grow guarded.
When they are treated with cruelty, they grow harsh.
But when they are treated with kindness, something opens.

Kindness doesn't just change moods.
 It changes culture.

A kind teacher shifts the tone of the whole classroom.
A kind manager makes a job bearable—even joyful.
A kind neighbor creates a street where people feel safe
(Thank you, Lou, of Hockaday Drive).

You won't always see the impact.
But that doesn't mean it's not happening.

People remember how you made them feel.
Your kindness may be the first kindness someone's
received in weeks.
You may never know how much it mattered.
But it does.

The Kindness You Don't See

Some of the most important kindnesses are invisible. They happen in the places no one claps for.

- The friend who answers the late-night call.

- The parent who chooses patience when exhaustion screams louder.

- The cashier who keeps smiling after someone's been rude.

- The stranger who holds a door for someone they'll never meet again.

These small acts?

They're the glue that holds our world together.

They don't go viral.
But they ripple.
They create pockets of safety.
And people who feel safe are more likely to pass it on.

Kindness is never wasted.
Even if it seems small.
Even if it's unseen.

Be Kind Because the World Is Hard

Some will tell you not to be kind because it makes you soft.
Because the world is cruel.
Because people will take advantage.

Be kind anyway.

Be kind because cruelty doesn't need more helpers.
Be kind because children are watching.
Be kind because the world is heavy, and you might be the
reason someone doesn't fall apart today.

Kindness doesn't fix everything.
But it creates moments of relief.
And in those moments, people can breathe again.

Final Thought

Kindness is not about being a hero. It's about being human.
Every day gives you a hundred chances to practice.
Take them.

Even if you're tired.
Even if you're scared.
Even if no one else is doing it.

Kindness is how we begin to build the world we deserve.
One choice.
One word.
One small act at a time.

Chapter 6: Listen Before You Judge

You might be wrong. And even if you're right, listening is still the kindest place to begin.

Before you decide who someone is, what they meant, or where they stand— listen.

This is not easy.

It's easier to assume.
It's faster to label.
It's more satisfying to judge.

But judgment, without listening, becomes a wall. And kindness cannot climb over that wall until you open a gate.

Listening Doesn't Mean Agreement

Listening is not surrender.
It is not compliance.
It is not an admission that the other person is right.

Listening simply says:
"I care enough about you—or the world we share—to hear what you're saying."

And that act alone can change the temperature in the room.

People raise their voices when they feel unheard.
People dig into opinions when they think no one's willing to understand.
People escalate when silence becomes the only option they're given.

When you listen, truly listen,
you give people a chance to soften.

The Danger of Deciding Too Soon

How many relationships have been ruined by things said
out of context? How many movements have been ignored
because their messengers didn't speak in perfect words?
How many people have we written off because they
reminded us of someone else who hurt us?

We decide who people are far too quickly.
And we are often wrong.

That doesn't mean you must excuse harmful behavior.
It doesn't mean you have to trust someone who's shown
you they're not safe.

But it does mean leaving room for complexity.

It means pausing before you assign motive.
It means choosing curiosity over certainty.

You might learn something.
You might still disagree.
But you'll come away stronger for having listened.

Listening as a Revolutionary Act

In a noisy, shouting world,
listening is rebellion.

Listening says:

"I will not be dragged into the chaos. I will meet this moment with presence."

Listening takes courage.
Because sometimes, you'll hear things you don't like.

Sometimes, you'll be challenged.
Sometimes, you'll change.

That's the point.

We do not listen just to be polite.
We listen to grow.

When You Don't Want to Listen

Some voices are hard to hear.
Some people are hard to face.
Some truths are uncomfortable.

But listening doesn't mean opening your ears to cruelty.

You do not owe space to someone who only wants to harm.
You do not have to sit quietly through abuse.
You do not need to tolerate hate disguised as "opinion."

Listening is for building bridges, not burning yourself.
Know the difference.

And when it's safe,
when it's possible,
when your heart can hold it—
choose to listen again.

The Power of Being Heard

Everyone wants to feel seen.
Everyone wants to feel known.

When you give someone your attention—without
interruption, without correction—you give them dignity.

And dignity changes people.

You may not agree with them.
You may not become friends.
But you may be the first person who treated them like a
human being, not a headline.

And that might be the first step toward something better.

Final Thought

Listen not because it's easy.
Listen because it's necessary.

Listen because change starts with understanding.
Listen because judgment without understanding is lazy.
Listen because silence leaves too much room for
resentment.

One of the most radical things you can do in this world is to listen with an open heart.

So start today.

Open your ears.
Close your assumptions.
And let someone else's story come through.

You might just become the person they never expected to find:
A good neighbor.
A safe place.
A willing ear in a world that too often shouts over the truth.

Chapter 7: Hurt People Need Help, Not Hate

When someone hurts you, the instinct is to hurt them back.
It's fast.
It's easy.
It feels fair.

But it doesn't heal anything.
It only spreads the pain further.

The truth is simple: hurt people hurt people. And if you respond to hurt with more hurt, the cycle stays alive. If you respond with something different—something unexpected—you have the power to stop it. That power lives in mercy. It lives in refusing to mirror the harm you've received.

Meeting pain with anger feels natural.
Meeting pain with patience feels nearly impossible.
But it's patience that changes things.

When someone lashes out, they are often asking a deeper question:
"Am I still worth something, even when I'm broken?"
"Will someone still see me, even now?"

You don't have to excuse cruelty.
You don't have to accept mistreatment.
But you can recognize that most cruelty comes from a place of fear, loss, or old scars.
Understanding doesn't erase accountability.
It simply refuses to add fuel to a fire that's already out of control.

In the House of the Good Neighbor, we believe that mercy is strength. We believe it is possible to hold people accountable without crushing them. We believe you can set boundaries without setting fires.

You can walk away from harm without carrying hatred. You can protect yourself and still wish someone else well. You can leave behind toxic spaces without letting bitterness take root inside you.

That is strength.
That is mercy.
And it's the only way the cycle of pain ever ends.

You will encounter people who test your patience. You will encounter people who seem determined to misunderstand you. You will encounter people so lost in their own pain that they can't see anything else.

The easy choice is to hate them back. To gossip about them. To hope they fail. To quietly celebrate when they stumble.

The harder choice—the better choice—is to wish them healing instead of harm. You don't have to stay close to people who keep hurting you. But you can walk away without hoping for their downfall. You can leave without carrying resentment like a badge of honor.

There's a kind of quiet power in choosing to help a hurting person instead of hurting them back.

It might be a small help:

A kind word when they expect a cruel one.
A simple act of patience when they deserve your anger.
A refusal to let your hurt harden you.

It's not about pretending their actions were right.
It's about deciding who you want to be.

Every time you choose mercy, you become a stronger version of yourself. You become the kind of person who makes healing possible—not just for others, but for yourself too.

Helping doesn't always mean staying. Sometimes the best help you can offer is distance. Sometimes helping means letting people face the natural consequences of their choices without shielding them. Sometimes it means saying, "I care about you, but I will not allow you to destroy me."

Mercy is not weakness.
Mercy can be fierce.
It can look like a quiet boundary drawn in permanent ink.
You can wish someone healing—and still refuse to let them drag you into their storm.

Both things can be true at once.

The next time someone's pain spills out onto you, remember:

You don't have to catch it.
You don't have to throw it back.
You can let it fall at your feet.
You can respond with strength, with clarity, with dignity.

You can choose to be a stopping point, not a continuation. You can say, "The pain ends here." And in doing so, you make space—for yourself and for others—to build something better.

Not everyone will recognize the mercy you show.
Not everyone will thank you.
Some will take advantage of it.
That's okay.

The value of mercy isn't measured by the reaction it gets. It's measured by the person you become when you offer it. You are not responsible for how others receive your kindness. You are responsible only for what you plant in the world.

Plant mercy.
Plant patience.
Plant hope.
Even if you never see the garden grow.

Hurt people will keep crossing your path.
You will keep facing choices: retaliate or restore, hate or help, harden or hope.
Every choice shapes you.

The House of the Good Neighbor is built by people who make the harder choice—again and again.
Not because it's easy.
Not because it guarantees success.
But because it's the only way to build a better world, one small act at a time.

The pain can stop with you.

And that choice—small, quiet, unseen—is how real strength looks.

Chapter 8: Be the Calm in the Storm

You don't have to match the storm around you. When people are loud, chaotic, frantic, or cruel, the world tells you to mirror it. Fight back. Shout louder. Strike first.

But there's another way.
You can be the calm in the storm.
You can choose not to be pulled under.
You can choose steadiness when everything else feels like it's unraveling.
You can choose patience when the easy option is panic.

Staying calm isn't ignoring the storm.
It's refusing to become part of it.

Being calm doesn't mean you're unaffected. It doesn't mean you don't care. It means you decide how you want to move through the chaos. It means you realize you can't control the weather around you—only the anchor within you.

You don't have to raise your voice just because everyone else is shouting. You don't have to rush your decisions just because others are panicking.

You can hold steady.
You can breathe slower.
You can choose to be different.

Calm is not weakness.
Calm is power, directed.

When you stay calm, you create an opening. In the middle of someone else's anger, your calm can invite peace. In the middle of someone else's fear, your calm can invite hope. In the middle of confusion, your calm can invite clarity.

It doesn't always happen immediately. But your presence matters more than you know. Most storms die down faster when they realize there's no one fueling them anymore. You can be the one who refuses to throw more wind into the storm.

Of course, calmness doesn't come naturally all the time.

Sometimes your heart will race.
Sometimes your hands will shake.
Sometimes you'll feel your blood boiling just like everyone else's.

Staying calm isn't about never feeling stirred up. It's about noticing the storm rising inside you—and deciding not to let it drive your actions. It's about practicing presence. Slowing your breathing. Grounding yourself before you open your mouth.

It's not always easy.
But it's always worth it.

In a fight, anyone can escalate.
In a crisis, anyone can panic.
But the ones who change the outcome are the ones who keep their footing.

When you stay calm:

You see options others miss.
You create solutions others can't imagine.
You protect your own energy so you can lead instead of getting lost.
You become a lighthouse in the dark—not by outrunning the storm, but by standing firm inside it.
Staying calm doesn't mean staying silent about what matters. There will be moments you need to speak.

Moments you need to act.
Moments you need to stand firm for what's right.

But even in those moments, calmness is your greatest strength. Calm doesn't mean stepping away from the battle. It means stepping into it with a clear mind and a steady heart.

You don't fight chaos with more chaos.
You fight it with focus.
You fight it by refusing to let anger choose your words for you.

Sometimes, the people who yell the loudest feel the most powerless. Sometimes, the people who move the fastest feel the most lost. Calmness isn't about judging them. It's about choosing not to lose yourself alongside them.

You might be the only steady voice they hear today. You might be the only steady presence they experience this week. That matters. Even if they don't realize it in the moment, it matters.

Your calmness is a gift you give to the people around you—and to yourself.

In your family.
In your friendships.
In your neighborhood.
In the world.

You will see storms rise again and again.
Big storms.
Small storms.
Storms made of fear, of anger, of hurt.

You can't stop every storm from coming.
You can't protect everyone from the winds.

But you can refuse to be one more voice of panic. You can choose to be the one who steadies the ship when the waves hit hardest. You can choose to be the person others can lean on, breathe with, and gather strength from.

The House of the Good Neighbor is built by people who learn how to stay steady when others crumble.
Not because we are stronger.
Not because we are smarter.
But because we decide:

"I will not be shaped by fear. I will not be driven by chaos. I will choose who I am, even when it's hard."

When the storm rages around you, plant your feet.
Breathe deeply.
Move slowly.
Speak clearly.
Be the calm.

You never know who might find their way because of it.

Chapter 9: Celebrate Differences Without Comparison

You were never meant to be like everyone else. And no one else was meant to be exactly like you. The world was designed to be different—messy, colorful, wildly varied. Yet somewhere along the way, we were taught that differences are threats instead of treasures.

That different means wrong.
That different means dangerous.
That different means less.
But that isn't true.
And deep down, you know it.

The beauty of a good neighborhood, a good life, a good world—is found in our differences, not in our sameness.

Comparison is a thief.

It sneaks in and convinces you that someone else's success diminishes your own.

That someone else's strength weakens you. That someone else's light casts a shadow on you. Comparison turns differences into weapons. It says:

"If they are beautiful, then maybe I am not."
"If they are strong, then maybe I am weak."
"If they belong, then maybe I don't."

But that's a lie.
Someone else's light doesn't dim yours.

There's room for all of it.
There always has been.

Imagine a world where everyone looked the same. Spoke
the same. Thought the same. Dreamed the same dreams.

It would be a quiet, colorless world.
A world without invention.
A world without creativity.
A world without surprise.
It's the tension between differences that makes life
beautiful.

The musician and the scientist.
The thinker and the builder.
The dreamer and the doer.
We need all of them.
We need all of us.

Celebrating differences means letting go of the need to rank
everything. Not every difference needs to be measured. Not
every difference needs to be judged. Different doesn't have
to mean better or worse. Sometimes different just means
different—and that's enough.

Celebrating differences means learning to be curious
instead of suspicious. It means asking questions instead of
assuming answers. It means letting yourself be surprised by
how much there is to learn from people who are not like
you.

Of course, celebrating differences isn't always comfortable. It stretches you. It challenges you. It forces you to admit that your way isn't the only way.

But that's where real growth lives—in the uncomfortable places. You don't have to agree with everything to respect it. You don't have to understand everything to honor it. You only have to recognize that every person you meet sees the world through a window you cannot fully look through—and that alone makes them worth listening to. The House of the Good Neighbor isn't built by people who look the same, think the same, or live the same.

It's built by people who believe that differences make us stronger. It's built by people who refuse to let fear choose their friendships. It's built by people who choose appreciation over competition. When you celebrate differences, you create space where everyone can show up fully, without shrinking, without editing themselves to fit into someone else's box. You create real belonging, not just surface-level acceptance.

It's easy to surround yourself with people who look and think exactly like you. It's harder—and better—to build friendships across differences. It's harder—and better—to stay in conversations with people who challenge you. It's harder—and better—to open your door wider, not narrower.

The world doesn't need more echo chambers.
The world needs more conversations across bridges.
You can be one of the bridge-builders.

When you celebrate differences, you also set yourself free.
Free from the pressure to be like everyone else. Free from
the endless, exhausting game of comparison.

You no longer have to outshine anyone. You no longer
have to prove your place by pushing someone else down.
You can simply be—yourself, fully and unapologetically.
And you can allow others to do the same.

When you stop competing, you start connecting.
When you stop comparing, you start celebrating.

The House of the Good Neighbor is built by people who
see beauty in every kind of face, in every kind of voice, in
every kind of dream. It's built by people who know that
community is not about erasing differences. It's about
weaving them together into something stronger, richer, and
more real than anything we could create alone.

Celebrate differences.
Cherish them.
Learn from them.
Let them make you bigger, not smaller.
The world doesn't need more mirrors.
It needs more windows.
Be the neighbor who builds windows.

Chapter 10: Always Make Room at the Table

A real community isn't built by accident.
It's built on purpose.
It's built by people who choose, over and over again, to make room for others.

It's easy to close ranks.
It's easy to stick with people who feel familiar.
It's easy to look at a full table and say, "We have enough."
But in the House of the Good Neighbor, the table is never too full to pull out another chair.
Making room at the table is not about charity. It's not about feeling good about yourself. It's about remembering what it feels like to be left out—and deciding you won't let someone else carry that feeling alone.

You know that feeling.
Everyone does.

The sideways glance that says, "You don't belong here."
The empty seat that stays empty even when you needed it most. You have the power to change that for someone else.
You have the power to make them feel seen instead of invisible.

Inclusion doesn't happen by accident.
It happens because someone looks around and says:
"Who's missing?"
"Who hasn't been invited?"
"Who's standing on the edges, hoping someone will notice them?"

It happens because someone decides that belonging isn't something you have to earn—it's something you are given, simply because you exist. You can be that someone. Every single day.

Making room at the table doesn't mean you'll always be comfortable. It means you're willing to stretch your idea of family, of friendship, of community. It means you're willing to be changed by who you let in. It means you're willing to make space for stories that don't sound like ours, for dreams that don't mirror your own, for voices that may not always agree with you.

That's not weakness.
That's real strength.

A community that only welcomes people exactly like itself is not strong—it's brittle.

It can be broken by the first gust of difference.

Sometimes making room is a small act:

Shifting your body to make space on a crowded bench.
Asking the quiet person at the edge of the group what they think.
Inviting someone new into a conversation, even when it's easier to stick with what's familiar.

Sometimes it's a bigger act:

Standing up when you see someone being excluded.
Creating opportunities for voices that often go unheard.

Building tables in spaces where there never were any. Big
or small, it always starts with noticing. Noticing who's
missing. Noticing who's waiting. Noticing who's hoping
someone will see them.
Making room doesn't mean losing yourself. It means
enlarging yourself. It means realizing that the table doesn't
get weaker when more people sit down—it gets stronger.

More perspectives.
More ideas.
More laughter.
More life.

When you make room, you aren't giving something away.
You're gaining something you didn't even know you
needed. You're gaining the chance to see the world through
someone else's eyes. You're gaining the chance to build
something bigger than you could ever build alone.
It will be tempting, sometimes, to close the table off.

Especially when you're tired.
Especially when you're hurt.
Especially when the world feels overwhelming.

It will be tempting to shrink your world down to the people you already know, the people who are already comfortable. Resist that temptation. Comfort zones don't build better worlds. Bigger tables do. Tables where people are messy and different and beautiful and challenging—and welcome anyway.

When you pull out a chair for someone, you're saying:

"There's space for you here."
"You matter."
"You don't have to fight to be seen—you already are."

That kind of welcome is rare.
That kind of welcome is powerful.
That kind of welcome can save a life.

You may never know how much it means to someone that you noticed them. You may never know what battle they were fighting before you made space for them. But kindness always matters, even if you don't see the harvest.

The House of the Good Neighbor is built by people who choose to make room. Even when it's inconvenient. Even when it's uncomfortable. Even when it costs them something.

It's built by people who believe that belonging is not a prize to be earned—it's a right to be shared.

So pull out the chair.
Slide over.
Wave someone in.

Build the kind of table where no one has to wonder if
there's space for them.

Because there is.
Because you made sure of it.

Chapter 11: Apologize When You Harm, Forgive When You're Hurt

Everyone makes mistakes.
Everyone says the wrong thing sometimes.
Everyone hurts people, even without meaning to.
That's not a flaw in being human.
That's part of being human.

What matters isn't whether you harm or get hurt—it's what you do next.

In the House of the Good Neighbor, we believe that community only survives when people learn to apologize and forgive. Not perfectly. Not easily. But consistently.

Apologizing well is a skill—and it's rare. Most apologies sound like defenses:

"I'm sorry you felt that way."
"I'm sorry if I did something wrong."
"I'm sorry, but—"

A real apology leaves no room for excuses. It says: "I hurt you. I see that. I'm sorry. How can I make it right?"

It takes strength to admit you caused pain. It takes even more strength to sit with that truth instead of running from it.

An apology doesn't erase the hurt.
But it opens the door to healing.

Apologizing doesn't mean you're weak. It doesn't mean you're worthless. It means you care more about the relationship than about protecting your pride. It means you believe the person you hurt is worth the discomfort it takes to face your mistake. It means you are choosing growth over ego. Apologizing is an act of respect—for the other person and for yourself.

It says: "I know I'm capable of better. And you deserve better from me."

On the other side, forgiveness is just as powerful—and just as hard. Forgiveness doesn't mean forgetting.

It doesn't mean excusing. It doesn't mean staying in situations that are harmful. Forgiveness means you refuse to let the hurt define you. It means you decide to stop carrying around the weight of someone else's mistake. Forgiveness is something you do for yourself as much as for the other person. It clears out the bitterness before it hardens into something you can't break free from.

Forgiving someone doesn't mean pretending it didn't happen.

It means you can remember it without letting it rot you from the inside out. It means you can wish them well, even if you need to create space. It means you can heal, even if they never apologize.

Forgiveness is a choice you make, often more than once. It's rarely a feeling that appears overnight. It's a decision you make again and again: "I will not let this pain turn me into someone I am not."

Apology and forgiveness are two acts that work together to repair the cracks between people.

Without apology, wounds stay open.
Without forgiveness, scars turn into walls.

Communities break down not because people make mistakes—but because they refuse to heal from them. When you choose to apologize when you harm, and forgive when you're hurt, you become part of the repair crew instead of the wrecking crew.

You become someone who builds trust instead of suspicion. You become someone who makes relationships stronger, not thinner.

It's tempting to wait for the other person to move first.
"I'll apologize if they do."
"I'll forgive when they finally say they're sorry."

But waiting keeps you stuck.
Sometimes you have to move first.
Sometimes you have to be the one who sets the chain reaction in motion. You might not get the response you

want. You might not see instant change. But doing the right thing is never wasted. It builds something strong inside you, even if the outside doesn't change right away.

When you apologize sincerely, you become safer for the people around you. You show them that mistakes don't end relationships. That honesty isn't dangerous. That vulnerability is allowed.

And when you forgive, you become lighter. You make more room inside yourself for joy, for connection, for new beginnings. Both acts—apology and forgiveness—are gifts. Not just to others, but to yourself.

They clear the air.
They clear the heart.
They make real closeness possible again.

The House of the Good Neighbor isn't a house without cracks or messes. It's a house where people are brave enough to fix what's broken.

Where people say, "I'm sorry." Where people say, "I forgive you." Not because it's easy. But because it's worth it.

Community isn't made out of perfection. It's made out of people who are willing to stay at the table, even when it's uncomfortable, even when it's hard.

So apologize when you harm. Forgive when you're hurt. And watch what grows when you choose to repair instead of retreat.

Chapter 12: Be the Neighbor You Needed When You Were Small

Think back to when you were younger. Think about the moments when you felt small, scared, or unsure. Think about the days when you needed someone—anyone—to notice you.

To believe in you.
To sit beside you when the world felt too big to handle alone.

You remember those moments. You always will. Now you have the chance to become the person you once needed. It's easy to think the world changes through big movements and bold gestures. And sometimes it does.
But more often, it changes because one person decides to show up when it matters most. One person decides to offer the kind of patience, kindness, and encouragement that could have made all the difference for them years ago.

You have the power to be that person.
You don't have to be perfect.
You just have to be willing.

Maybe you needed someone to listen without rushing you.
Maybe you needed someone to see your potential when you couldn't see it yourself.
Maybe you needed someone to show you that you were lovable, even on your worst days.
Whatever you needed—be that.

For your friends. For your family.

For the stranger who crosses your path at exactly the right moment.

Kindness doesn't erase the hard things from our past.
But it can rewrite the story for someone else.

Being the neighbor you needed isn't always grand or obvious. It's often quiet. It's often simple. It looks like remembering someone's name when you didn't have to. It looks like holding space for someone's fear without making them feel weak. It looks like celebrating someone's small victories when the world only seems to notice the big ones.

It looks like becoming a safe place.
And safe places are rare—and sacred.

You know what it feels like to wish someone would stand up for you. Now you can stand up for others.

You know what it feels like to wish someone would include you. Now you can pull someone into the circle.

You know what it feels like to wish someone would believe you were enough, exactly as you were. Now you can say that to someone else—and mean it.

You can break cycles.
You can start new ones.

You can create the kind of space you once needed most.

Some days you'll get it right.
Some days you'll miss your chance.

That's okay.

This isn't about getting every moment perfect. It's about paying attention. It's about living with your heart open enough to notice when someone needs what you once needed. And then doing something about it—even if it's small. Especially when it's small.

Small acts of love are never wasted.
They echo longer than you will ever know.

Maybe you needed more encouragement.
Maybe you needed more patience.
Maybe you needed someone to tell you it was okay to fail and try again.

What you needed most is a clue to what you are called to give.

That need shaped you. It taught you how it feels to be unseen—or seen. It gave you a roadmap for how to show up for others with more empathy, more tenderness, more grit.

Use it.
Turn that old ache into a new kind of generosity.

You don't have to wait for the perfect moment.
You don't have to wait until you feel ready.
You don't have to fix everything for everyone.
You just have to keep showing up—with patience.
With presence.

With the kind of stubborn hope that says, "Someone did this for me—or someone should have—and now I will." The kindness you give now isn't just a gift to others.

It's a healing for yourself, too. It's a way of telling your younger self, "You mattered then. You matter now."

The House of the Good Neighbor isn't built by people who forget what it feels like to be small. It's built by people who remember—and choose to live differently because of it. It's built by people who decide to be the voice of encouragement they once longed to hear.

The steady hand they once reached for.
The open door they once wished someone would hold for them.

You can be that neighbor.
You can be that light.
And every time you are, the world becomes a little softer, a

little stronger, a little more like the place you once dreamed it could be.

Chapter 13: Defend Peace, But Don't Fear the Fight

Peace is worth protecting.
Kindness is worth protecting.
People are worth protecting.
But protection doesn't always look like softness.

Sometimes it looks like standing up. Sometimes it looks like saying no. Sometimes it looks like stepping between harm and the vulnerable.

Being a good neighbor doesn't mean avoiding conflict at all costs. It means knowing when to step forward—and how.

There's a difference between loving peace and fearing conflict. One is a choice rooted in strength. The other is a reaction rooted in fear. You don't defend peace by pretending everything is fine when it's not. You don't defend kindness by allowing cruelty to run unchecked.

There will be times when you must speak. Times when you must act. Times when you must draw a line and say, "This is not okay." And you can do it without becoming what you are standing against.

Strength doesn't mean shouting.
Strength doesn't mean tearing others down.
Strength doesn't mean being fueled by rage.

Real strength is quiet inside.
Real strength is knowing who you are—and refusing to be dragged away from it.

You can stand firm without becoming cruel. You can protect without becoming hard. You can fight for good without losing your goodness. That's the harder fight. And it's the one that matters most.

Sometimes defending peace means stepping in when others stay silent. It means calling out injustice when it would be easier to look away. It means protecting someone who can't protect themselves. It means choosing to be uncomfortable rather than complicit.

It's not always dramatic. It's often quiet. A steady refusal to accept cruelty as normal. It's a hand reaching out. It's a voice saying, "This isn't right." It's a heart brave enough to stay soft even when the world grows sharp.

You won't always feel brave when you step up. Your hands might shake. Your voice might crack. You might question yourself. That's okay. Courage isn't the absence of fear. It's moving forward even when fear whispers at your heels. Defending peace requires courage—courage to protect what's good without destroying yourself in the process. Courage to stay human when anger tries to make you forget who you are.

Not every battle is yours to fight. Part of wisdom is knowing when to step in—and when to step back. You don't have to fight every argument.

You don't have to win every debate. Choose your battles with care. Save your strength for the fights that matter. Fighting every small thing leaves you exhausted. Saving your strength for real injustice makes you effective.

The goal is not to win.
The goal is to protect.
The goal is to heal.

Sometimes the fight is loud. Sometimes it's quiet. Sometimes defending peace looks like standing between two people in conflict. Sometimes it looks like quietly standing with someone who is being left out.

Sometimes it's a protest.

Sometimes it's a conversation. Sometimes it's a decision not to give up hope, even when it's easier to become cynical.

Defending peace happens a hundred ways a day. You don't have to do it perfectly. You just have to keep showing up. Anger has a short shelf life. It burns hot—and burns out fast.

Love lasts longer.
Love builds.
Love outlasts the noise.

When you fight, fight from love, not from rage. Fight because you care too much to stay silent. Fight because you believe kindness is worth defending. And when you fight, never let the fight change who you are at your core.

Stay steady.
Stay human.
Stay grounded.

The House of the Good Neighbor isn't built by people who love peace at the expense of justice. It's built by people who are willing to defend peace when it matters most. It's built by people who know that being good doesn't mean being passive. It means standing strong—with heart, with clarity, and with relentless hope.

So defend peace. Speak up. Step forward.

But do it without losing the very thing you're fighting for. And remember: the best fights leave more room for love—

Chapter 14: The Person vs The Cart Corral

They say character is what you do when no one is watching. If that's true, then the shopping cart might be one of the best tests of all. Because here's the truth: returning a shopping cart is easy.

It's quick. It's harmless. It's simple. And no one gives you a medal for doing it.

But that's the point. You're not doing it to be seen. You're doing it because it's the right thing to do.

Because someone has to gather those carts. Because a cluttered parking lot can scratch someone's car or block someone's path. Because we all share the same space—and every choice matters.

When you leave your cart in the middle of the lot, you're saying, "Someone else will deal with it."

When you take it back, you're saying, "I'll take responsibility for what I used."

It's that simple. And that profound.

This isn't about carts. It's about mindset. It's about respect.

It's about being the kind of person who takes ownership of their small actions—because they understand those small actions shape the world.

Let's be honest—sometimes it's raining. Sometimes your kids are in the car. Sometimes your back hurts.

But even then, there's usually someone nearby who can use a little help. You can offer to take someone's cart once they're done loading their groceries. You can wait patiently away from them and as soon as they've loaded the last bag say, "I'll take that for you." And you can push it all the way back inside—even if you don't need one yourself.

These little moments stack up. They build a neighborhood, one cart-length at a time.

We live in a world where so many people are waiting to be inspired. Waiting for a leader. Waiting for a movement.

But what if the movement is just…returning your cart? What if it's checking on your neighbor? Holding the door? Saying thank you? Picking up trash that's not yours? What if changing the world begins in the parking lot?

That's the heart of the House of the Good Neighbor. It's easy to complain about how selfish people have become. It's harder—but more powerful—to live in a way that proves them wrong.

When you return a cart, no one claps. No one posts your picture. But something inside you grows stronger.

You become someone who finishes things. Someone who doesn't leave a mess for the next person. Someone who chooses order over chaos, care over convenience.

Every time you walk that cart to the corral, you are telling the world: "I don't need a spotlight to do the right thing."

And that—more than any speech or slogan—is the foundation of neighborliness. Because doing good is not a performance. It's a practice.

There's something quiet and dignified about taking that walk back to the cart return. In that moment, you are not important. You are not impressive. You are simply kind. And that is exactly what this world needs more of.

This chapter isn't about guilt. It's about invitation. An invitation to remember that your smallest actions carry weight. To remember that when you do something kind—without applause—you keep something sacred alive. To remember that while the world races ahead, sometimes the best thing you can do is slow down... and walk the cart back.

You won't get a reward. You won't trend. But you will matter. Because the cart corral is a symbol. A mirror. A tiny, ordinary test that reflects something bigger:

Are you the kind of person who sees something out of place—and puts it back where it belongs? Are you the kind of person who doesn't wait for thanks to do the right thing?

In the House of the Good Neighbor, we believe this:

The little things aren't little. They are the bricks that build a culture of kindness.

So return your cart. Take someone else's. Be the person who moves quietly through the world, making it better— not louder.

Because what you do when no one is watching…

Might just be the truest thing about you.

Chapter 15: How to Handle Losing

You will lose. You will fail. You will fall short of what you hoped would happen. If you care enough about anything about people, about justice, about community—there will be times when your best effort won't be enough to win the day.

And that hurts. It's supposed to hurt. But losing isn't the end. Losing is where real strength begins.

We are taught to hate losing. To fear it. To avoid it at all costs. Winning is celebrated. Losing is buried and ignored. But losing well is one of the most important things you will ever learn how to do.

Because losing well teaches you how to stand back up. How to rebuild when you're tired. How to stay kind when you're disappointed. How to keep believing when you have every excuse to give up.

Losing strips away the extra. It forces you to ask yourself: "Who am I when things don't go my way?" "Who am I when I am not being praised or celebrated?" It reveals what you're really made of—not when you succeed, but when you don't. If you only stay kind when you're winning, you were never truly kind. If you only stay patient when the outcome favors you, you were never truly patient. Character is proven in loss, not in victory.

When you lose, feel it. Don't bury it. Don't fake a smile if you don't feel one. Let yourself grieve the thing you wanted but didn't get.

There's no strength in pretending you don't care. Strength is feeling the weight of the loss—and deciding to carry on anyway. Strength is choosing to believe that even if today didn't end the way you hoped, tomorrow is still worth showing up for.

Handling loss doesn't mean minimizing it. It doesn't mean convincing yourself it didn't matter. It means learning to carry disappointment without letting it turn into bitterness. It means holding onto hope—not a shallow hope that everything will always be easy, but a stubborn hope that says, "This loss doesn't get the final word." It means building a resilience that is quieter than anger and deeper than pride.

You will see other people gloat when you lose.
You will see people who celebrate your setbacks.
Let them.

The loudest celebrations of your loss are not proof that you were wrong. They are proof that what you stood for scared them. If you lose for the right reasons, you have not really lost. You've simply planted a seed that hasn't grown yet. Keep planting.

Handling loss well also means refusing to let shame take root. You are not a failure just because you failed. You are not worthless because something you built broke apart. Loss is feedback, not identity. You can learn from it. You can adjust your course. You can come back stronger, clearer, and even more determined. But only if you don't let the loss convince you to quit altogether.

In the House of the Good Neighbor, losing is not shameful. It is expected. It is respected.

Because anyone who tries to make the world better will run into walls. Anyone who fights for something bigger than themselves will lose battles along the way. It's not about never losing. It's about refusing to lose your heart in the process.

There will be days when you fall.
There will be days when you wonder if it's worth it.
There will be days when you feel alone.
But you are not alone.

Every neighbor who ever fought for something true, something kind, something beautiful—lost something along the way. And every one of them who kept going made it possible for someone else to stand taller.

You are part of that same story.
Lose if you must.
Fall if you must.
But stand back up.
Smile if you can.
Grit your teeth if you have to.

And keep moving toward the house we are building together.

One step.
One act.
One imperfect, unstoppable heart at a time.

Chapter 16: Losing Someone You Love

One of the hardest truths in life is this: Everyone you love is temporary. Including you.

No matter how tightly we hold onto each other, eventually, we have to let go. Death isn't fair. It isn't clean. It doesn't always come with goodbyes wrapped neatly in words we wish we had said. Sometimes it just takes. And leaves us standing there, aching in ways we didn't know were possible.

People like to say, "They're in a better place."

But here was the better place.
Here, where they laughed.
Here, where they rolled their eyes and hugged too tight and told terrible jokes and sang off-key.
Here, where their hand brushed yours.
Here, where they sat across from you with coffee and tired eyes and plans for tomorrow.
Here was the miracle.

Not somewhere else. Not later. Now. Here.
This was the better place.

Loss is sharp because it mattered. Because they mattered. It should hurt. It should leave a mark. That's the price of connection: If you dare to love deeply, you risk breaking deeply too.

And it's worth it. It will always be worth it. Even when the silence after them feels unbearable. Even when the days stretch longer than you know how to handle. It was worth it.

The way to honor the people we lose isn't by pretending we aren't broken. It isn't by pretending we didn't want more time. The way to honor them is to carry them forward in how we live. In how we listen. In how we show up for others. In how we love, knowing full well that loving means losing someday—and doing it anyway.

We carry them by becoming the kind of people they were proud of. By building something they would have believed in.

Cherish the people while they're here. Don't wait for tomorrow to say the thing you're scared to say. Don't assume they know how much they mean to you. Don't put off the small celebrations, the long conversations, the simple moments.

One day you will wish for just one more ordinary afternoon. One more bad joke. One more story you've heard a thousand times but would give anything to hear again. If you have the chance to love someone today, take it. Fully. Out loud.

Grief never really ends. It just changes shape. It becomes a part of the landscape you carry. Some days it feels like a mountain. Some days it feels like a stone in your pocket.

It's not weakness to still hurt after months, after years. It's not failure to still miss them at random times, in random places. It's a sign that they mattered. And you are still capable of loving what you cannot touch anymore.

There is no replacement for the people you lose. There is only space they carved out in you—a space you can choose to fill with gratitude, with memory, with meaning.

You will still laugh.
You will still build new dreams.
You will still find joy.
It doesn't erase the loss.

But it weaves the pain into a bigger story. A story where love mattered more than fear. Where connection mattered more than certainty. Where saying goodbye hurt, but loving in the first place mattered more. If you are hurting, let yourself hurt.

You don't have to rush it. You don't have to explain it. You don't have to get over it by a certain date. There is no timeline for missing someone who mattered.

There is only this: You loved. You lost. And somehow, you are still here.

Still loving. Still trying. Still honoring their life by living yours with as much courage as you can.

The House of the Good Neighbor is not just for the living. It's a house built by every act of kindness we learned from those who came before us. Every lesson they gave us. Every moment they shaped without even knowing it. They are stitched into the walls. They are woven into the table we keep making bigger. They are written into the blueprint, forever.

This was always the better place. And because they were here—because you are here—it's better than it would have been without them.

When Someone You Know Loses Someone They Love

You don't need perfect words. There aren't any. When someone is grieving, your job is not to fix the pain. It's simply to stand near it—without turning away.

You can say: "I'm so sorry for your loss." "I'm here for you."

That's enough. That's more than enough. Because in grief, it's not advice that heals. It's presence. It's love that doesn't try to tidy up the mess.

So don't worry about the speech. Don't overthink the message. Just show up. Stay kind. And be willing to sit in silence if that's what they need.

That's what good neighbors do.

Chapter 17: Let Kids Be Kids

Children are not mini adults. They're not here to meet our expectations or carry our regrets. They are here to learn, to stumble, to play, to grow.

Childhood is not supposed to be a boot camp for adulthood. It's supposed to be the one time in life when wonder wins out over worry. Protect that wonder. Don't make them earn it.

Many of us were raised with shouting, hitting, humiliation. Maybe it "worked." Maybe we "turned out fine."

But fine isn't good enough. We can do better. Pain shouldn't be passed down like an inheritance.

Breaking the chain doesn't mean you're soft. It means you're strong enough to build something different. It means you have the guts to stop repeating what hurt you.

Corporal punishment is not discipline. It's domination. It doesn't teach right from wrong. It teaches fear, shame, anger.

You cannot beat good character into someone. You can only grow it—carefully, patiently—like a seed.

If your child fears you, they are not learning respect. They are learning that love can hurt. And that's a lesson no child deserves.

There's no such thing as a bad kid.

There are hurting kids. Overwhelmed kids. Abandoned kids. Scared kids.

And they don't always have the words to explain it.

So they act out. They test boundaries. They push and pull because they don't know how else to say: "Please help me."

Get on their level. Get low. Get quiet. Look past the behavior and listen for the message underneath.

There is no shame in therapy. There is no weakness in asking for help.

Therapy is not about turning kids into robots or "fixing" them. It's about giving them tools most of us never had. Tools to feel their feelings without drowning. Tools to speak instead of lash out.

Therapy isn't punishment for being "bad." It's a gift for learning to survive.

Don't mistake small bodies for small problems.

Kids carry stress—heavy, real stress—and they don't always know how to set it down.

School pressure. Friend drama. Family tension. Feeling misunderstood. All on top of just trying to figure out who they are.

When you add more anger, more demands, more judgment, you aren't toughening them up. You're burying them.

Be the safe place. Not the extra weight.

It feels good to step in. To tie the shoes. Solve the homework. Smooth every bump.

But when you do everything for your child, you aren't helping them. You're telling them you don't believe they can do it themselves.

Let them struggle. Let them fall sometimes. Let them learn they are strong enough to stand back up.

Rescue feels good in the moment. But resilience lasts a lifetime.

Your child does not belong to you. They are not a trophy. They are not a reflection of your image. They are a whole, separate, beautiful being.

You are here to guide them, protect them, support them. But not to control them.

Love that smothers becomes a prison. Love that respects becomes a launchpad.

It's easy to demand obedience. It's harder to teach character.

Obedience crumbles the minute no one's watching. Character stands up even when it's hard.

Teach them how to think, not just how to follow. Teach them why kindness matters, not just that "we say sorry."

Teach them that respect isn't about fear—it's about seeing the humanity in someone else. Real growth comes from understanding, not punishment.

Every moment you choose patience over rage, you are building a future.

Every time you choose conversation over hitting, you are changing a life.

You may not see the fruit of it today. You may not even see it in your lifetime.

But the world your children inherit will be shaped by the love, freedom, and courage you dared to give them now.

The Small Teachers Among Us

Let kids be kids—wild and weird,

Grass-stained knees and stories smeared.

Across their shirts and through the dirt,

With laughter loud and feelings hurt.

Let them climb and fall and try,

Let them ask the endless why.

Let them spin beneath the sky

With dreams too big to justify.

Let them chase what has no name,

Let them lose and start again.

Let them cry and let them roar—

They're not broken, they're just more.

More alive than we remember,

Hearts on fire, not cooled to ember.

They're the questions we once asked,

Before we learned to wear our mask.

We build fences, they dig holes.

We count minutes, they chase souls.

We stay safe—they dive in deep.

We hold grudges—they forgive in sleep.

So let's pause and watch them grow.

Let their wonder teach us slow.

Let their giggles shake our fear.

Let their bravery draw us near.

Because they are not just what comes next—

They are reminders we forget:

That life is not a list of tasks,

But joy we find when no one asks.

Let kids be kids—and let them show

How to be human, how to glow.

Then dare yourself, like they still do,

To play, to hope, to start brand new.

Chapter 18: Giving Without Expecting

Volunteering is one of the few things in life that is pure. It's giving with no paycheck waiting. It's showing up when you don't have to. It's helping without having anything to gain.

And that's exactly why it matters. In a world obsessed with getting, volunteering is one of the last sacred acts of giving.

When you volunteer, you have to get out of your own way. It's not about feeling like a hero. It's not about taking pictures or collecting compliments.

It's about showing up and asking, "What needs to be done?" Then doing it. Quietly. Faithfully. Even when no one thanks you. Especially then.

Wealth isn't measured by the money in your account. It's measured by what you do with the time you have.

Time is your most valuable currency. When you spend it helping someone who can never repay you, you are investing in something bigger than yourself. And unlike money, that investment never loses value.

People are carrying burdens you can't see. Some are drowning and smiling at the same time. Some are surviving hour by hour.

Volunteering doesn't erase their struggles. But it reminds them they are not invisible.

Sometimes, being noticed is the first step toward being saved.

You don't have to build a hospital. You don't have to cure a disease. Sometimes the smallest kindness is the lifeline someone needs. Fixing a fence. Delivering a meal (even through a delivery service). Sitting with someone who is grieving. Listening.

Small things stack up. And over time, they build a world that's less cold, less lonely, less cruel.

Volunteering pulls you out of your bubble. It shatters the idea that your life is the center of the universe. It humbles you.

It teaches you gratitude without lectures. It sharpens your heart the way lifting sharpens muscle—slow, steady, real.

You don't volunteer because you're better than anyone else. You volunteer because you're no better than anyone else.

Not every volunteer story is neat. You will face hard things. Awkward things. Ugly things. And you'll realize you can't fix everything.

But volunteering isn't about fixing the world overnight. It's about standing in the middle of the mess and saying, "I'm still here. I'm still trying."

That's real courage.

Help people without making them feel small. Give without expecting their loyalty, their praise, their performance.

Don't turn your giving into a debt they owe. True volunteering is about freedom—not charity that comes with invisible chains.

If you give, let it be a gift that expects nothing in return.

You can tell kids a thousand times to be kind. Or you can let them watch you roll up your sleeves and help someone.

You can tell them the world needs compassion. Or you can show them what compassion looks like in real life.

The lessons that stick aren't spoken. They're lived.

If the world feels harsh, volunteer. If people feel selfish, volunteer. If hope feels small, volunteer.

The world you want to live in won't build itself. It will be built by hands like yours—open, willing, steady.

You don't have to save the whole world. But you can save a corner of it. And that's enough.

Chapter 19: The Door You Said You'd Never Open

There are doors we bolt shut, heavy with hurt, sealed with promises we made to protect ourselves:

"Never again."

"Not after that."

"Not them."

And maybe we needed those promises once. Maybe they kept us standing when the world felt too sharp, too cold, too loud.

But promises made in pain aren't meant to be the walls we live behind forever.

One day, you'll walk by that door again— the one you swore you'd never touch.

You'll pause.

You'll feel the old hurt rise, hot and certain. But you'll feel something else, too— something softer.

A pull you didn't expect.

Forgiveness isn't forgetting. Forgiveness isn't pretending. Forgiveness is opening the door, not because they deserve it, but because you deserve peace.

It's saying: "You don't get to hold my heart hostage anymore."

Sometimes, opening the door isn't about rebuilding a relationship. It's about releasing the weight. It's choosing to let go of the story you've been telling yourself over and over and over again.

You're not weak for forgiving.

You're not foolish for being open.

You're just done letting old pain write today's script.

You get to decide what lives with you.

You get to decide what stays locked out.

You get to decide when the door opens again.

Some people will never apologize. Some will never understand the harm they caused. But you don't need their understanding to begin healing.

Forgiveness is not dependent on their growth. It's dependent on your desire to stop carrying what was never yours to hold forever. You can say, "That was real. That was painful." And still say, "But I choose something better now." You don't owe anyone access to your life. But you do owe yourself freedom.

The door doesn't open all at once. It creaks. It protests. It lets in light slowly, sometimes painfully. And you might flinch.

You might take one step and stop. That's okay. This is not a race. This is your heart, and it deserves your care. Maybe all you do is peek through the crack. Maybe all you do is sit nearby, letting the memory come and go. Even that is a form of movement. Even that is a kind of healing.

There's courage in the opening. Even if no one sees it. Even if no one says thank you.

You don't need an audience to heal. You don't need permission to move on. You just need honesty. And the quiet belief that you're allowed to live lighter than you've been.

Let go of the idea that you have to fix everything to move forward.

Some relationships stay broken.

Some chapters end mid-sentence.

You can still be whole.

Sometimes, the person on the other side of that door is family. Sometimes it's an old friend. Sometimes it's you.

We don't always realize how much resentment we hold against ourselves. We punish ourselves for mistakes we made with less wisdom, less strength, less support.

And that door? The one you never open? Sometimes it leads to your own forgiveness.

You are not the same person you were then. You are not frozen in the past. You have learned. You have grown. You are allowed to forgive who you were, who they were, and choose peace without pretending everything was okay.

Choosing peace is not pretending. It's just refusing to be held back. You won't always be met with warmth when the door opens. Sometimes it's empty on the other side. Sometimes it's still sharp. Sometimes the person isn't ready.

But the act of opening still matters. Because it changes you. It lets in air. It lets in light. It reminds you that even when the world tries to harden you, you still have a soft place inside.

And that place is sacred.

Mister Rogers said, "Forgiveness is a strange thing. It can sometimes be easier to forgive our enemies than our friends. It can be hardest of all to forgive people we love."

And yet, forgiveness is where we become most human. Most generous. Most brave.

The door you said you'd never open? It's still there. It's yours to choose. No pressure. No deadline.

Only this: When you're ready, you'll know.

And the house of the good neighbor will still be standing—waiting, welcoming, forgiving, just like you.

Chapter 20: You Have to Cheer for Yourself

No One Can Believe For You

People can encourage you.
They can tell you you're talented, kind, strong.
They can believe in your potential.
But it's not enough.

You have to believe it, too.
You have to be the one who bets on yourself
when no one else understands the dream you're chasing.

The World Will Try to Shrink You

The world is full of people who gave up.
People who settled.
People who traded their spark for comfort.
They will tell you to stay small because your hope reminds
them of what they lost.
Don't listen.
Don't dim yourself just because it makes someone else
more comfortable.
Your light is not a threat.
It's a beacon.

Faith In Yourself is a Skill

Faith in yourself isn't magic.
It's not something you're born with.
It's a skill you build, day by day.
Every time you keep a promise to yourself—
you sharpen it.

Every time you get back up after falling—
you strengthen it.
You don't wait for faith.
You build it.

Talk to Yourself Like Someone You Love

We are crueler to ourselves than we would ever be to a
friend. We call ourselves names we would never say out
loud. That has to stop.

Talk to yourself with the same kindness you would offer
someone you love.

Not because you're perfect—
but because you're trying.
And trying deserves kindness.

Trust Your Path, Even If It's Weird

Your journey might not look like anyone else's. It might
not fit neatly on a timeline or a checklist. Good.
It means you're writing something original.

Trust the strange turns.
Trust the slow seasons.
Trust the things you feel called to, even if no one else sees
it yet. Especially then.

Success Isn't Always Loud

Sometimes believing in yourself doesn't look like winning trophies.
Sometimes it looks like showing up when you're tired.
Sometimes it looks like quietly surviving a day that almost broke you.
Success isn't always loud.
Sometimes it's invisible.
But you know it.
You feel it.
And that's enough.

"There are three ways to ultimate success: The first way is to be kind. The second way is to be kind. The third way is to be kind." ~ Fred Rogers

Applaud Yourself for the Small Things

Celebrate the small wins.
The ones no one else notices.
The time you spoke up when it was scary.
The time you said no when you usually say yes.
The time you started over instead of giving up.
You are not waiting to be proud of yourself.
You can be proud right now.
Don't Wait for Permission

You don't need anyone's permission to chase your dreams.
You don't need anyone's approval to be proud of yourself.
Waiting for validation is a game you'll never win.

Live your life like you already have permission—
because you do. You always have.

You Are the Constant

People will come and go.
Circumstances will rise and fall.
Praise will find you, and then leave.
Criticism will sting, and then fade.
But you?
You are the only one who will live with your choices, your
dreams, your efforts, forever.
Be the one constant that cheers yourself forward.

If You Don't Believe, Who Will?

If you don't believe in your voice,
how can you expect the world to listen?
If you don't believe in your kindness,
how can you expect the world to feel it?
If you don't believe in your future,
how can you expect it to grow?
You are your first fan, your longest fan, your loudest fan.
 Be brave enough to stand in your own corner—
 no matter what.

Chapter 21: How to Know

How do you know if you're a good person? Not by the awards you've won. Not by your social media likes, your job title, your ability to say the right thing in front of the right people.

Being a good person is quieter than that. More invisible. More consistent.

It's not a declaration. It's a practice. And it begins with a simple, hard-to-answer question: "Do I care about the impact I have on others?"

Goodness doesn't come from guilt. It comes from awareness. When someone else is hurting, do you notice? When someone is excluded, do you speak up? When you could make someone's day a little lighter, do you do it? It's not about fixing the world in one grand gesture. It's about taking responsibility for the world that's right in front of you. Goodness is active. Not passive. It moves. It checks in. It tries.

Sometimes, we confuse goodness with niceness. But niceness is about being liked.

Goodness is about being honest.
Goodness tells the truth even when it's uncomfortable.
Goodness sets boundaries even when it's hard.
Goodness chooses the right thing, not the easy thing. Being good doesn't always feel good.
And it doesn't always get applause.
But it always leaves the world stronger than it was before.

Here's a harder truth:

Good people sometimes get it wrong. They snap.
They assume. They judge. They act out of fear or pain or
fatigue. But what makes someone good isn't that they never
fail. It's that they return.

They apologize.
They ask, "How can I be better?"
They listen.
They try again.

Goodness is not something you own. It's something you
choose, again and again. It's in how you speak to people
who can't help you. It's in how you behave when no one is
watching. It's in how you treat the waiter, the cashier, the
janitor. It's in how you drive when someone cuts you off.
It's in the jokes you make, the grace you give, the silence
you break. It's not perfection. It's direction. And every day,
you get to decide what direction you're going.

You won't always feel like you're doing enough. You'll
wonder if you're missing something important. You'll feel
overwhelmed by the weight of it all.

That's okay. Good people aren't superheroes. They're not
martyrs. They're ordinary people who make room in their
lives for someone else's needs.

They pause.
They notice.
They show up.
That's enough.

Don't let the world's definition of success confuse you. Big doesn't mean better. Loud doesn't mean right. Famous doesn't mean important. Some of the kindest, strongest, most important people you'll ever meet will never be on a stage. They'll be in the background. Quietly doing good.

They'll be the reason someone kept going.
They'll be the reason someone felt seen.
That matters more than you'll ever know.

How do you know if you're good? Check your habits. Check your tone. Check your patience when things go wrong. Check the way people feel after spending time with you. Do they feel lighter? Do they feel safe? Do they feel heard?

Those aren't feelings you can fake. They come from real goodness. The kind that comes from doing the work, not just saying the words.

Sometimes, the question isn't "Am I good?" It's "Am I willing to grow?" Because goodness isn't a fixed trait. It's something you expand into.

You learn more.
You mess up less.
You stretch.
You soften.
You get sharper and gentler at the same time.
You don't stop asking questions.
You don't stop learning.
You don't stop showing up.
That's what good people do.

If you're still reading this, it means you care. It means
you're trying. It means you're paying attention. And that,
more than anything, is what the world needs.

Not perfect people. Not self-righteous people. Not always-
right people. Just people who care enough to keep
becoming. To keep choosing good when it would be easier
not to. To keep saying: "I may not always get it right, but
I'll never stop trying."

That's how you know.
That's who you are.

Welcome home.

Chapter 22: You Are Worth Saving

There's a myth that healing looks like perfection. That once you begin to grow, the mess vanishes, the hurt fades quietly, and suddenly you're new. But that's not how it works. Healing is raw. It's painful. It's honest.

It's not about fixing you. You were never broken.
It's about stopping the run. Stopping the lie. Stopping the grin that says, "I'm fine," when your insides are burning down.

It's about dragging the old wounds out where you can actually see them — instead of pretending they don't hurt anymore. It's about saying what you swore you'd never say. Letting someone hear the ugliest parts of you — and finding out they don't run.

Therapy is standing in your own wreckage, hands bleeding, heart shaking, and saying, "I'm still here."

It's not easy. It's not pretty. It's not fast. But it's real. And real is better than perfect.

Healing doesn't have a highlight reel. It has missed calls, quiet tears, awkward truths, and moments where you wish you could go back to not knowing. But forward is the only honest direction.

You don't go to therapy because you're weak. You go because you're sick of carrying your past like it owns you. You go because you're tired of faking it for people who never learned how to see beneath your mask. You go because something inside you says, "Enough."

Enough pretending.
Enough stuffing it down so deep it spills out in other ways — in short tempers, cold shoulders, and restless nights.

You go because you're ready to stop surviving and start living. Even if your hands still shake. Even if your voice still breaks. You go anyway.

You go because staying stuck is more painful than moving through the fire. Because the hurt you avoid only grows heavier, while the hurt you face becomes something you can carry.

It takes courage to sit down and say, "I need help."
It takes guts to look a stranger in the eye and hand them the tangled, fragile mess of your life.

But in that moment — in that raw, terrified moment — you begin again.

Not by erasing your past,
but by learning how to carry it differently.
Not by becoming someone new,
 but by uncovering who you were before the shame took over.

Healing doesn't mean the pain never existed. It means the pain no longer controls you. It means your story has more than one chapter. It means you can write something new, even if the old pages still ache.

Some days, healing will look like deep, honest breakthroughs. Other days, it will look like simply getting out of bed.

Both matter.
Both count.

The voice that says you're too broken? It lies.
The voice that says you waited too long? It lies.
The voice that says you'll never get better? It lies.

You are not too late.
You are not too damaged.
You are not beyond repair.

You are human.
You are trying.
You are worth saving.

You don't owe anyone your healing timeline.
You don't have to explain why it still hurts.
You don't have to perform your progress to prove it's real.

Your healing is yours.

Quiet. Private. Powerful.

And every step you take — every time you sit down with the pain instead of running from it — you reclaim a little more of yourself.

Some people won't understand. That's okay.
Some people will question your journey. That's okay too.
Healing isn't about proving anything to them.

It's about becoming the version of yourself who no longer hides from the hard things. It's about living with both hands open — one holding your past with tenderness, the other reaching for what's next with hope.

You finally know what no one could tell you:

You are not too far gone.
You are not too much.
You are not a mistake to fix.
You are a story still being written.

And this chapter — the one where you choose to keep going — might be the most important one of all.

You are worth saving.
You always were.
You always will be.

Chapter 23: Strength Without Cruelty

Somewhere along the way, the story got twisted. Strength became about fists. About rage. About dominance. We started praising the loudest, the angriest, the cruelest, like being feared was the same thing as being respected.

It's not.

Fear fades. Fear breeds resentment. Fear doesn't build anything worth keeping.

Hurting others doesn't make you powerful. It makes you destructive. Anyone can break something. Anyone can tear down, rip apart, ruin. Real strength is the ability to build when it's easier to destroy. Real strength is protecting, not punishing. Violence might win the moment. But it loses the soul.

Mercy isn't softness. Mercy isn't weakness. Mercy is power under control. It's having every right to hurt — and choosing not to. It's standing strong enough in yourself that you don't need to prove it with fists or screams. Mercy is a hand reaching out instead of a fist swinging down.

Dominance is an empty crown. If you have to crush others to stand tall, you were never standing tall to begin with. You were standing on broken backs. And one day, they'll stop carrying you. Strength isn't about how many people you can push down. It's about how many you can lift without losing yourself.

Anyone can explode. Anyone can throw a punch, pull a trigger, shout someone down. It's the easiest thing in the world to lash out. But peace — real peace — takes more courage. It takes more self-control. It takes more vision.

It's harder to stand calmly when the world demands a fight. It's harder to choose healing over harm. That's why real peacekeepers are the strongest people you'll ever meet.

Peace isn't passivity. It's not rolling over, letting injustice win. Defending peace sometimes means standing your ground. Sometimes it means fighting — but fighting for something, not against everyone.

There are times when you must speak. Times when you must act. Times when you must draw a line and say, "This is not okay." And you can do it without becoming what you are standing against.

The real test isn't whether you can hit back harder. It's whether you can hold your ground without becoming what you hate. Can you face anger without adding to it? Can you face cruelty without mimicking it? Can you face fear without spreading it?

Strength isn't measured in scars given out. It's measured in scars carried with honor — the ones you earned for refusing to turn into something you despise.

It's time to stop worshiping bullies. It's time to stop confusing cruelty for leadership. It's time to stop clapping for the loudest, meanest voice in the room.

Bullies are not strong. They are scared. They are small. They roar because they are hollow.

Real strength is quiet. Real strength doesn't need to humiliate anyone to feel alive.

If we want a better world, we have to teach it. We have to raise children to see that gentleness is power. That kindness is resistance. That empathy is armor.

Teach them that a strong back is important, but a soft heart is just as vital. Teach them that defending peace is noble, but starting wars for pride is shameful. Teach them that real heroes don't leave ashes behind. They leave gardens.

Strength isn't the absence of fear. It's facing fear and choosing to be better anyway. Strength isn't about being untouchable. It's about being open enough to feel — and strong enough to keep standing.

You were made to be more than a weapon. You were made to be a protector. A builder. A defender of better things.

Defend peace. Don't fear the fight. And never mistake cruelty for courage.

Chapter 24: Healthy Food, Healthy Mind

What you eat is not just fuel. It's instruction. It tells your body how to heal, your brain how to think, and your spirit how to feel.

Your body listens to what you feed it. So does your mind. Every bite is a message. Strength or fatigue. Focus or fog. Clarity or confusion.

And here's the truth: you can't outthink your biology. You can't lecture your body into feeling better while handing it processed junk and pretending it doesn't matter.

We've made food a reward, a punishment, a distraction. But food is none of those things. Food is care. Food is energy. Food is your foundation.

Eating well isn't about being trendy. It's about being in tune. It's a quiet way of saying, "I'm worth it."

You wouldn't feed your dog candy for breakfast. You wouldn't pour soda into your car's gas tank. But we do it to ourselves—day after day.

We've also been sold a lie that junk food is "treating yourself." But feeling bloated, foggy, and inflamed isn't a treat. It's a trap.

Real self-care isn't wrecking yourself for a brief pleasure. It's choosing what builds you—especially when nobody's watching.

This doesn't mean every meal needs to be perfect. It means most meals should be honest. You know when you're feeding your future, and when you're feeding your momentary craving. Honor that knowledge.

Here's something worth considering: explore vegetarianism—or at the very least, make vegetables the star of your plate.

A plant-rich diet isn't just good for your body. It's good for the planet. It's good for animals. It's good for your long-term health.

Vegetables aren't side characters. They're the main event. They bring color, life, nutrients, and power.

Try it. Add a vegetarian day each week. Swap meat for lentils, beans, or tofu in one meal. Explore a vegetable you've never cooked before.

The truth is: your body thrives on clean, simple, whole foods. It feels lighter, faster, sharper.

The mind you want—the calm, focused, energized mind—is built at the table. It's not just about calories. It's about chemistry. About clarity. About care.

Start small. Add a green thing to your plate. Drink water before your coffee. Cook one more meal at home.

Small steps become habits. Habits become lives. And a life built on nourishment is a life that holds up even when things get hard.

Here's the best part: food can be joyful. This isn't about giving things up. It's about gaining energy, focus, and health.

Cooking is a way of loving yourself.

Sitting down to eat without distraction is a way of telling your body, "You matter."

Your body isn't asking for gourmet meals. It's asking for attention. For balance. For honesty.

Healthy eating is an act of gratitude. It says: Thank you to your body for carrying you. Thank you to your brain for dreaming. Thank you to your heart for beating another day.

And when you start saying thank you to your body, your body starts saying thank you back. In energy. In strength. In lightness.

Don't fall into the trap of waiting until your health breaks to start paying attention.

Don't wait for burnout to drink water.
Don't wait for anxiety to stop with the sugar.
Don't wait for brain fog to ask where the greens are.

You are allowed to feel good now. But it starts with what you feed the system that holds you together.

If there's one thing to take from this chapter, it's this: Your body deserves better than what our culture calls "normal."

Normal is fast food. Normal is sugar highs and crashes.
Normal is skipping meals, then bingeing.
Normal is not working.

Let's build a new normal. Let's build it one honest plate at a time. Eat with intention. Eat with curiosity. Eat like someone who has a life to live and a mind to sharpen.

You don't have to go vegan overnight. But try a vegetarian meal. Try three. Try more.

Respect your body like you'd respect your child. Like you'd respect your best friend. Like you'd respect your neighbor.

Because you are your first neighbor. And the way you feed yourself is the way you treat yourself.

Start there. With care. With greens. With water. With the choice to give yourself a better chance.

Because you're worth it. You always were.

"I don't want to eat anything that has a mother."

~ Mister Rogers

Chapter 25: The Fire You Carry

Anger isn't evil. It's a fire. And like fire, it can warm or it can burn. It rises when something we love is threatened, when something sacred is broken. It demands attention, but it doesn't always deserve control. The question isn't, "Do you feel anger?" The question is, "What will you do with it?"

Most of us are taught to either fear our anger or be ruled by it. But there's a third way. A better way. You can *listen* to your anger without being led by it. You can *name* it without unleashing it. Anger is a signal — a flare shot from the heart. Don't ignore it. Don't worship it. Understand it.

Ask it questions. Why are you here? What are you defending? What are you afraid of? What pain are you covering up? Most anger isn't pure rage. It's grief with nowhere to go. It's fear that doesn't know how to speak. It's sadness in armor. Get underneath it. That's where healing begins.

Anger has energy. It's real, and it's powerful. But it doesn't have wisdom on its own. That's your job. That's where you come in. You are the one who decides what shape that fire takes. Will it be a torch that guides? Or a blaze that destroys? Your future depends on the answer.

The world will give you plenty to be angry about. Injustice. Cruelty. Betrayal. Hypocrisy. But if you let your anger be louder than your values, you'll forget what you're fighting for. And when you forget what you're fighting for, you start to fight just to fight. That's when fire becomes poison.

In the House of the Good Neighbor, we don't shame anger. We shape it. We build something from it. Movements are born from fire, but they must be built with care. Speak with clarity, not cruelty. Act with focus, not frenzy. Let your fire move you — but let your *character* decide where you go.

Not all battles deserve your flame. Some fights are distractions. Some people are fire-starters looking to pull you into their chaos. Don't waste your heat proving your worth to people who aren't even listening. Save your fire for the work that matters — the building, the healing, the protecting.

You don't have to be calm to be kind. You don't have to be quiet to be wise. You just have to be *intentional.* That's the work. Let your anger fuel your steps, not dictate them. Let it remind you what matters — and then let your deeper values take the lead.

Your fire is not your enemy. It's part of you. But it is not *all* of you. You carry empathy too. You carry love. You carry the ability to pause, to question, to redirect. Every time you do, you prove that you are stronger than whatever tried to break you.

So hold the fire. Don't deny it. But hold it with care. Let it warm you. Let it move you. Let it light the way. But never let it become your identity. You were made for more than burning. You were made to build. Even in anger. Especially in anger.

Light the way forward — not the world on fire.

Chapter 26: Choose Your Attitude

You can't control everything that happens. But you can control how you walk into the room. And that might just change everything.

We are not always taught that attitude is a choice. Often, we're told to "calm down," "cheer up," "just let it go," or "be positive." These phrases come like pop songs in a storm — catchy, but useless.

But choosing your attitude doesn't mean ignoring your feelings. It means giving them a seat at the table — and not letting them drive the car.

The Myth of Automatic Reactions

Some will say, "I can't help how I feel."
And that's true — at first.

Feelings rise like weather. You don't schedule them. You don't control the moment they arrive. But just like the weather, you can choose how you prepare and respond. You can carry an umbrella. You can pause instead of reacting. You can turn a gust of wind into a deep breath.

What you can control is what comes next.

You may feel frustration, but you can choose not to speak with cruelty. You may feel hurt, but you can choose not to pass that pain on to someone else. You may feel ignored, but you can choose to ask for connection rather than shut down.

That choice — the choice of your attitude — is one of the most powerful acts of personal strength and social kindness you will ever practice.

Your Opinion Is Not Always Your Final Answer

Here's a truth that might surprise you: You don't have to keep every opinion you've ever had. In fact, you shouldn't.

Opinions are not sacred. They are tools. And like any tool, they can be sharpened, changed, or put down. Sometimes, we form opinions from fear. From a small piece of the story. From what someone told us before we had the full picture.

And sometimes, we hold onto those opinions because we've mistaken them for personality.

But you are allowed to stop and ask:

"Is this belief helping the people I care about?"
"Is this attitude serving the world I want to live in?"
"Is this the version of myself I want to carry forward?"

We all want to be right. That's human. But being kind, being open, being constructive — those things will matter more in the end.

Not Just What's Best for You — What's Best for the Outcome

When choosing how to feel, how to respond, how to be — don't only ask, "What feels good right now?"

Ask:

"What will lead to healing?"
"What creates peace?"
"What brings understanding, not just comfort?"

If you've been wronged, anger might feel good. But clarity might do more. If you're misunderstood, defensiveness might be your instinct. But curiosity might open a door. If someone's hurting near you, pity might rise first. But compassion and action will go further.

The attitude you choose isn't just for you — it affects everyone around you.

And in a world where moods spread like wildfire, your decision to choose grace, patience, or humor might be the thing that turns someone else's entire day around.

Let Your Feelings Come…

Then Let Your Wisdom Decide

This chapter is not asking you to be emotionless. Quite the opposite. Your emotions are vital. They are alarms, songs, roadmaps, signals of truth. But they are not always wise on their own. That's where you come in.

Let the anger arrive — but ask it what it wants to protect.
Let the sadness arrive — but ask it where the wound is.
Let the joy arrive — but ask it how to share the light.

And then decide, with intention, how to respond.

This is not about perfection. It's about direction.
It's about reminding yourself that you get to steer the ship, even if the waters are rough.

A Story of Choosing Light

Once, I was certain someone was trying to embarrass me. They made a comment in front of others — not cruel, but sharp. It cut. I could feel my chest tighten. My mind began writing the script: They don't respect me. They think I'm a joke. I should say something back. Loud. But I paused. I let the moment sit.

Instead of reacting, I said something light. I gave them the benefit of the doubt. I moved on.

Later, that person pulled me aside. They apologized. They told me they were nervous, and trying to connect, and it came out wrong. We ended up talking for an hour about real things. That wouldn't have happened if I'd chosen my first reaction.

I'm not proud because I "held back." I'm proud because I chose who I want to be — not just how I felt in a moment.

That's what this chapter is really about.

This House Believes in the Power of Pause

The House of the Good Neighbor doesn't expect you to be emotionally perfect. It simply asks you to pause. To give yourself space between reaction and response. To use your attitude like a tool, not a shield.

To remember:

Your mood can hurt someone. But it can also heal them.
Your attitude can start a fight. But it can also start a movement.
Your words can close a door. But they can also open one.

The choice is yours.

Closing Thought

So today — and every day — choose.

Choose how you feel with purpose.
Choose how you speak with care.
Choose how you think with love.

You won't get it right every time. But if you keep trying… you'll keep making this world a better place to be.

Chapter 27: Face What You'd Rather Avoid

Change does not come from comfort.

It comes from discomfort you're finally willing to face.

The truth is, most of us want change. We just don't want confrontation. We want healing — but we don't want to open old wounds. We want justice — but we don't want to rock the boat. We want progress — but we don't want discomfort.

You don't have to like confrontation. But you do need to learn how to walk through it with purpose.

And here's the secret: It's not about being loud. It's about being clear.

What Are You Avoiding?

You already know the answer. The text you haven't sent. The truth you haven't spoken. The pattern you haven't broken. The apology you haven't made. The boundary you haven't set.

Avoidance pretends to be peace. But really, it's just postponing the storm. And sometimes the longer you wait, the harder the lightning strikes.

If you want to live a life of real integrity — the kind that feels good in your chest when you're alone — you have to stop avoiding the very moments that are asking for your courage.

Start Small — But Start

You don't need to solve everything in one day. But you do need to start. Start with a sentence. Start with "Can we talk?" Start with "I've been carrying something." Start with "This is hard for me to say."

Start before you're ready. Start while your voice still shakes. Start while the door is open.

Courage isn't the absence of fear. It's the decision to show up anyway.

It's Okay If They React

We avoid confrontation because we fear how others will respond. They might get defensive. They might cry. They might disagree. That's okay. Their reaction doesn't mean you were wrong to speak. It means they're human, too.

We can't control how others feel — but we can speak from a place of truth and care.

We can stay calm. We can stay kind. We can stay grounded in the reason we showed up in the first place: because something needs to change.

It's Not About Winning

This is not a war. You don't need to win. You need to be understood. And to understand.

That's what confrontation is at its best — not a fight, but a bridge. It's an invitation.

To grow.
To shift.
To be honest.
To be better.

Come to it with openness, not armor. You are not here to defeat them. You are here to find what's true.

When You've Been Silent for Too Long

If you've held your feelings for weeks, months, or years, know this: They haven't disappeared. They've just gone underground. They come out in resentment. In tone. In withdrawal. In distance. It's not too late to speak. You may have waited too long for the "perfect" moment, but now you have the honest one. Use it.

Say:
"I should have said this sooner."
"I didn't know how."
"I've changed since then."

Give your truth a path to walk out on.

The Risk of Saying Nothing

Avoiding confrontation might feel safer — but it's a slow kind of damage. When you stay quiet, you're not avoiding pain. You're allowing it to stretch out indefinitely.

You're letting small harms grow big. You're letting misunderstandings become walls. You're letting moments pass that could have changed everything.

Say the thing. Even if it's messy. Even if it's awkward. Even if it's late. Say the thing.

Be Brave Enough to Stay Kind

You can be honest and kind. You can be direct and gentle. You can be upset and still be loving.

Don't confuse confrontation with cruelty. You don't need to raise your voice. You don't need to throw blame. You don't need to storm out.

You just need to stay in the room. With your values intact. With your heart steady. With your words clear.

Kindness during conflict is not weakness. It's strength refined.

A Script for the First Step

"I care about you. That's why I need to say this."
"This has been sitting on my heart."

"I'm nervous to bring it up, but I need to."
"I'm not trying to hurt you. I'm trying to be honest."

Use your own words. But let them be rooted in care, not control. And if you're confronting something in yourself, say it inward:

"I'm ready to stop running."
"I can't avoid this anymore."
"I want to change."

The first words don't have to be perfect. They just have to be true.

The House Asks You to Be Brave

The House of the Good Neighbor is not a house of silence. It is a house of truth. Of care. Of uncomfortable growth. We don't ignore what's broken. We fix it. We don't run from what hurts. We face it. We don't avoid hard conversations. We learn how to have them.

If you want a better world, you will have to confront what keeps it stuck. If you want peace, you will have to speak.

If you want growth, you will have to risk discomfort.

So take the step. Face the thing. Say the words.

Be the kind of neighbor who doesn't let things rot in silence. Be the one who dares to bring light into the dark corners.

You are not here to stay comfortable. You are here to make things better. Even if that starts with something hard.

Chapter 28: Beware the Echoes: Living Wisely with Social Media

Social media is not free. It doesn't charge your bank account. But it often charges your peace, your time, and your trust in others.

You scroll for connection but walk away agitated. You tap for news but leave uncertain. You open the app for a moment—and suddenly, an hour has passed, and your mood has changed.

This is not an accident. It's the design.

The Game of Telephone, Digitized

Remember playing telephone as a kid? One person whispers a message down the line, and by the end, the story is twisted and laughably wrong.

Now imagine millions of people whispering, reposting, rewording, and remixing—except no one's laughing. They're angry. They're scared. They're convinced.

That's the digital echo chamber. That's how lies spread faster than truth. That's how people become strangers to their neighbors.

Your Emotions Are the Product

Social media platforms make money when you stay engaged. And what makes people stay engaged?

Outrage. Fear. Drama. Conflict.

Your most reactive self is the one the algorithm wants. Not your wisest, kindest, most reflective self—but your most clickable self. The one who clicks on the scary headline. The one who shares the meme without checking the facts. The one who argues in the comments.

It's not because you're weak. It's because the system is strong—and built to be addictive.

No Source Has a Monopoly on Truth

Even major networks—yes, the ones we grew up trusting—now rely on clickbait.

Headlines are designed to provoke, not inform. Clips are cut short to spark rage, not clarity. Algorithms reward drama, not depth.

So what do you do? You diversify.

You never rely on one source alone. You question. You verify. You slow down your reactions. And most importantly, you remember: not everything deserves your attention.

The Gift of the Bubble

When the noise becomes too loud, there is no shame in turning it down. My mother once said, "It's okay to live in your own little bubble." At the time, it felt like retreat. Now, it feels like wisdom.

There is power in choosing peace. There is health in choosing stillness. There is clarity in stepping outside the endless scroll and remembering what's real:

Your breath. Your family. Your hands. Your neighborhood.

You're Allowed to Pause

You don't have to know everything. You don't have to be caught up. You don't have to comment on every story, every tragedy, every scandal.

You are allowed to take a break. You are allowed to delete the apps. You are allowed to unsubscribe.

Silence is not ignorance. Sometimes, it's healing.

Connection vs. Contagion

Social media promised connection. But what it often delivers is contagion. Not of viruses, but of moods. Anxieties. Outrages. Misinformation. Mistrust.

So ask yourself:

"Is this post helping me become who I want to be?"
"Is this conversation making me more open or more bitter?"
"Is this thread building bridges—or burning them?"

You are not helpless in this. You can choose how you engage.

Start Small. Reclaim the Real

Instead of doom-scrolling for two hours, take a walk.
Instead of arguing with a stranger, check in on a friend.
Instead of reacting to everything, reflect on something.

The internet is loud. But your soul doesn't have to be.

Make Room for Real Life

The best parts of life don't live in your feed. They live in
kitchens and porches and books and playgrounds and eye
contact. Make room for what's real. Make room for what's
right in front of you. And when the world online feels too
heavy to carry—don't. Put it down.

Walk outside your bubble and realize: it's not as small as
they made it seem. It's exactly the size you need.

Final Thought

You're not wrong for using social media. You're not
foolish for getting caught in its spell. We all have. But you
are wise to notice it. You are strong to set boundaries. You
are kind to protect your peace. The internet is a tool—not a
home.

Build your home where your values live. And when the
noise gets loud, step back into your bubble. Not to hide, but
to heal.

Thank you, Mom.

Chapter 29: How to Start Building Your Own House

(With the Heart of the Good Neighbor)

You've made it this far—not just through a book, but through a belief system. Through a call. Through a challenge. You're here because something inside you knows: the world can be better.

And it starts right where you are.

You don't need permission. You don't need a certification. You don't need to get everything right. You just need to begin.

Let's start building.

Start With One Brick

Every house begins with one brick. Every movement starts with one choice. Don't wait for the grand gesture. Don't wait until you feel ready. You won't.

Return the cart. Check on your neighbor. Tell someone you're proud of them. Leave the angry comment unsent. Donate what you can. Volunteer somewhere. Anywhere. Be the first to say sorry. Invite someone new to your table. Listen longer. Judge slower.

Pick a brick and place it. Today. Right now.

Use What You Already Have

You don't need more money, more time, more influence to get started. You need heart. You need consistency. You need willingness.

What talents do you have? Use them. What time can you carve out? Give it. What love are you holding back? Share it. Start your house with what's already in your hands.

Let Your House Be Imperfect

The House of the Good Neighbor is not a mansion. It doesn't need gold trim or clean white walls. It needs truth. It needs effort. It needs soul.

Don't worry if you mess up. You will. Don't abandon the mission because someone criticized it. They will. But keep building anyway.

Bring Others In

A house is never truly a home until others feel welcome inside it.

Let people see how you live. Let them ask questions. Let them challenge you. Let them bring bricks of their own. This house isn't just yours—it's ours. And it grows stronger when more hearts are involved.

Start a kindness club. Create a support group. Start conversations. Share this book. Host a dinner where everyone brings a story. Make room.

Listen More Than You Speak

This house is built with humble tools. One of them is listening.

Listen to children. Listen to those who've been silenced. Listen to people you don't agree with—not to debate, but to understand. Listening isn't weakness. It's construction.

Every voice you make space for is another beam that holds this place up.

Make Maintenance a Habit

Houses fall apart when they're ignored. So will your efforts. Check in with yourself. Recommit. Make your values visible. Post them. Say them. Practice them. Let people hold you accountable. Sweep the floors of bitterness. Patch the holes made by gossip. Replace what no longer serves.

This is living, breathing work.

Let the Bubble Help You, Not Hide You

My mother once said, "Live in your bubble." And she was right. You can't save the world if you're constantly consumed by its noise.

Social media will pull you in with rage and despair. News will cycle fear on repeat. Step away when you need to. Your mental peace is not a betrayal—it's preservation.

Use the bubble not to block the world out, but to heal so you can reenter it stronger.

The House You Build Will Outlive You

The chair you pulled out, the kindness you offered, the child you supported—they ripple. You may never see the final shape of the house. But your hands shaped it.

Let that be enough.

And if you ever wonder if it's worth it—if any of this is reaching anyone—remember: someone is always watching. Someone is learning from you. Someone is holding on because of what you chose to do.

Keep building.

The Blueprint Is Yours Now

There are no more chapters after this one. No more instructions. Because now the pages belong to you.

Write your own.

Build your House of the Good Neighbor—messy, human, beautiful—and never stop letting love be the reason you keep showing up.

We'll be building right alongside you.

www.ingramcontent.com/pod-product-compliance
Lightning Source LLC
Chambersburg PA
CBHW071219090426
42736CB00014B/2888